PIANO | VOCAL | GUITAR ▪ CD   VOLUME 105

Piano Play-Along

BEE GEES

T0050662

Cover photo: © Michael Putland / RetnaUK / Retna Ltd. USA

ISBN 978-1-4234-9805-6

HAL•LEONARD®
CORPORATION
7777 W. BLUEMOUND RD. P.O. BOX 13819 MILWAUKEE, WI 53213

Visit Hal Leonard Online at
www.halleonard.com

CONTENTS

HOW CAN YOU MEND
A BROKEN HEART

Words and Music by BARRY GIBB
and ROBIN GIBB

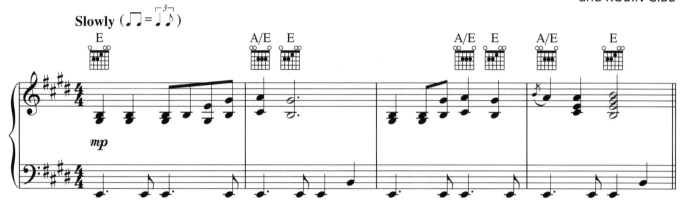

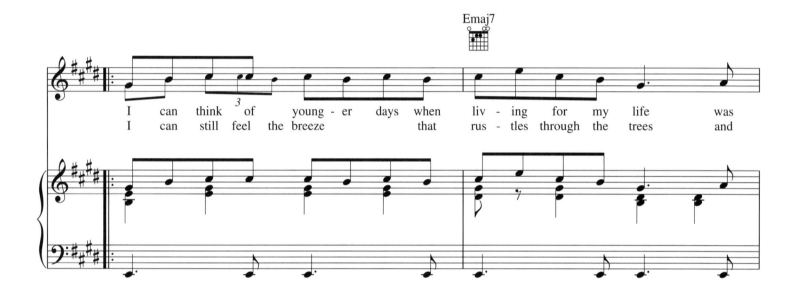

I can think of young-er days when liv-ing for my life was
I can still feel the breeze that rus-tles through the trees and

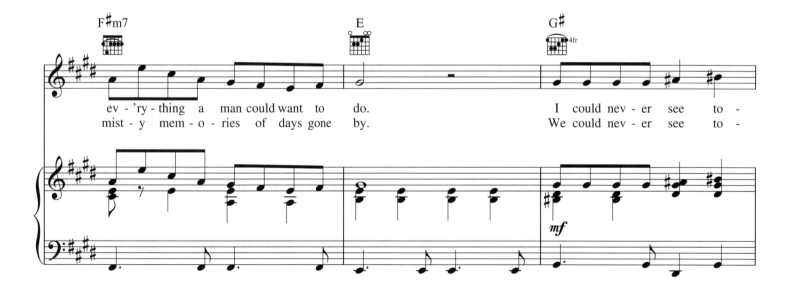

ev-'ry-thing a man could want to do.   I could nev-er see to-
mist-y mem-o-ries of days gone by.   We could nev-er see to-

HOW DEEP IS YOUR LOVE

Words and Music by BARRY GIBB,
ROBIN GIBB and MAURICE GIBB

I STARTED A JOKE

Words and Music by BARRY GIBB,
ROBIN GIBB and MAURICE GIBB

JIVE TALKIN'

Words and Music by BARRY GIBB,
ROBIN GIBB and MAURICE GIBB

Moderately, with a strong beat

It's just your jive talk-in', you're tell-in' me lies, __ yeah; jive talk-in', you wear a dis-guise. __ Jive talk-in', so mis-un-der-stood, __ yeah; jive talk-in', you're

NIGHT FEVER

Words and Music by BARRY GIBB,
ROBIN GIBB and MAURICE GIBB

Moderate Disco beat

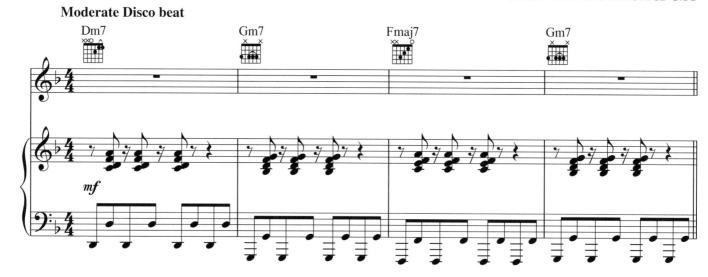

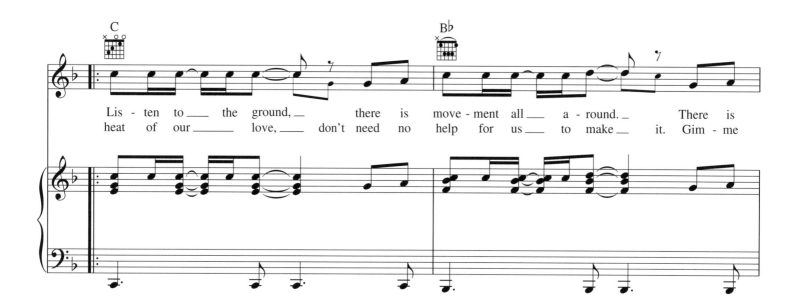

Lis - ten to ___ the ground, ___ there is move - ment all ___ a - round. ___ There is
heat of our ___ love, ___ don't need no help for us ___ to make ___ it. Gim - me

some - thing go - in' down, ___ and I can ___ feel it.   On the
just e - nough ___ to take ___ us to the morn - in.'   I got

STAYIN' ALIVE

Words and Music by BARRY GIBB,
ROBIN GIBB and MAURICE GIBB

Ah, ha, ha, ha, stay-in' a - live, _ stay-in' a - live. _ Ah, ha, ha ha,

stay-in' a - live. _____

_ Well now, I _

Life go - in' no - where. ____

NIGHTS ON BROADWAY

Words and Music by BARRY GIBB,
ROBIN GIBB and MAURICE GIBB

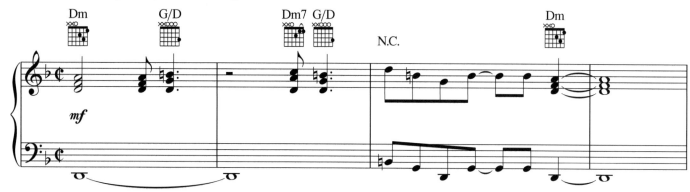

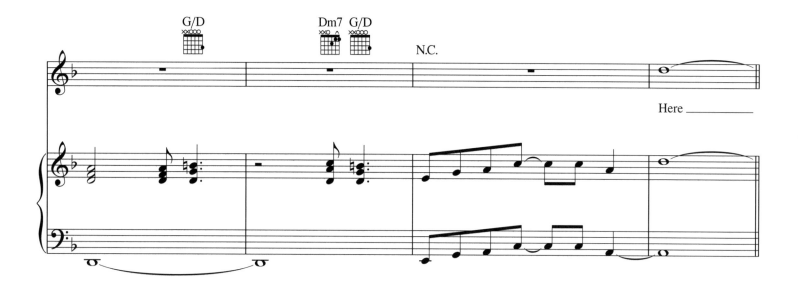

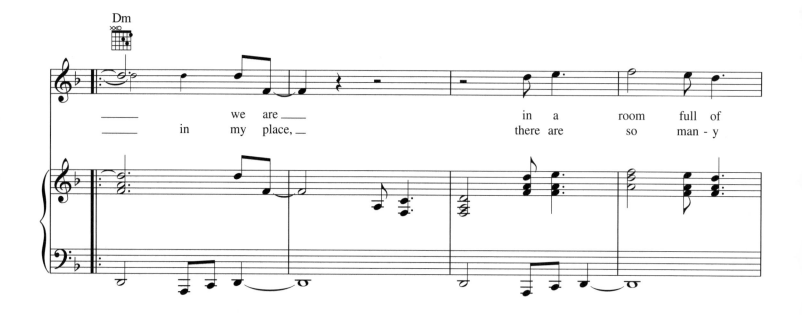

YOU SHOULD BE DANCING

Words and Music by BARRY GIBB,
ROBIN GIBB and MAURICE GIBB

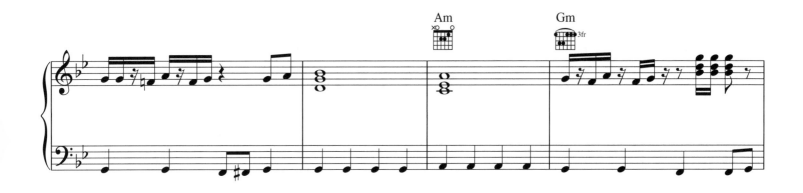

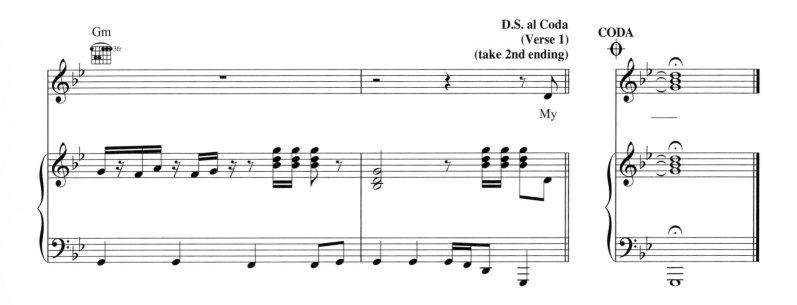

THE ULTIMATE SONGBOOKS

HAL•LEONARD
PIANO PLAY-ALONG

These great songbook/CD packs come with our standard arrangements for piano and voice with guitar chord frames plus a CD. The CD includes a full performance of each song, as well as a second track without the piano part so you can play "lead" with the band!

1. MOVIE MUSIC
00311072 P/V/G $14.95

2. JAZZ BALLADS
00311073 P/V/G $14.95

3. TIMELESS POP
00311074 P/V/G $14.99

4. BROADWAY CLASSICS
00311075 P/V/G $14.95

5. DISNEY
00311076 P/V/G $14.95

6. COUNTRY STANDARDS
00311077 P/V/G $14.99

7. LOVE SONGS
00311078 P/V/G $14.95

8. CLASSICAL THEMES
00311079 PIANO SOLO..............$14.95

9. CHILDREN'S SONGS
0311080 P/V/G $14.95

10. WEDDING CLASSICS
00311081 Piano Solo..............$14.95

11. WEDDING FAVORITES
00311097 P/V/G $14.95

12. CHRISTMAS FAVORITES
00311137 P/V/G $15.95

13. YULETIDE FAVORITES
00311138 P/V/G $14.95

14. POP BALLADS
00311145 P/V/G $14.95

15. FAVORITE STANDARDS
00311146 P/V/G $14.95

17. MOVIE FAVORITES
00311148 P/V/G $14.95

18. JAZZ STANDARDS
00311149 P/V/G $14.95

19. CONTEMPORARY HITS
00311162 P/V/G $14.95

20. R&B BALLADS
00311163 P/V/G $14.95

21. BIG BAND
00311164 P/V/G $14.95

22. ROCK CLASSICS
00311165 P/V/G $14.95

23. WORSHIP CLASSICS
00311166 P/V/G $14.95

24. LES MISÉRABLES
00311169 P/V/G $14.95

25. THE SOUND OF MUSIC
00311175 P/V/G $15.99

26. ANDREW LLOYD WEBBER FAVORITES
00311178 P/V/G $14.95

27. ANDREW LLOYD WEBBER GREATS
00311179 P/V/G $14.95

28. LENNON & McCARTNEY
00311180 P/V/G $14.95

29. THE BEACH BOYS
00311181 P/V/G $14.95

30. ELTON JOHN
00311182 P/V/G $14.95

31. CARPENTERS
00311183 P/V/G $14.95

32. BACHARACH & DAVID
00311218 P/V/G $14.95

33. PEANUTS™
00311227 P/V/G $14.95

34 CHARLIE BROWN CHRISTMAS
00311228 P/V/G $15.95

35. ELVIS PRESLEY HITS
00311230 P/V/G $14.95

36. ELVIS PRESLEY GREATS
00311231 P/V/G $14.95

37. CONTEMPORARY CHRISTIAN
00311232 P/V/G $14.95

38. DUKE ELLINGTON STANDARDS
00311233 P/V/G $14.95

39. DUKE ELLINGTON CLASSICS
00311234 P/V/G $14.95

40. SHOWTUNES
00311237 P/V/G $14.95

41. RODGERS & HAMMERSTEIN
00311238 P/V/G $14.95

42. IRVING BERLIN
00311239 P/V/G $14.95

43. JEROME KERN
00311240 P/V/G $14.95

**44. FRANK SINATRA –
POPULAR HITS**
00311277 P/V/G $14.95

**45. FRANK SINATRA –
MOST REQUESTED SONGS**
00311278 P/V/G $14.95

46. WICKED
00311317 P/V/G $15.99

47. RENT
00311319 P/V/G $14.95

48. CHRISTMAS CAROLS
00311332 P/V/G $14.95

49. HOLIDAY HITS
00311333 P/V/G $15.99

50. DISNEY CLASSICS
00311417 P/V/G $14.95

51. HIGH SCHOOL MUSICAL
00311421 P/V/G $19.95

52. ANDREW LLOYD WEBBER CLASSICS
00311422 P/V/G $14.95

53. GREASE
00311450 P/V/G $14.95

54. BROADWAY FAVORITES
00311451 P/V/G $14.95

FOR MORE INFORMATION,
SEE YOUR LOCAL MUSIC DEALER,
OR WRITE TO:

HAL•LEONARD®
CORPORATION
7777 W. BLUEMOUND RD. P.O. BOX 13819
MILWAUKEE, WISCONSIN 53213

Visit Hal Leonard Online at
www.halleonard.com

Prices, contents and availability
subject to change without notice.

Hal Leonard
ANTHOLOGY SONGBOOKS

These collections set the gold standard for 100 prime songs at an affordable price.

All titles arranged for piano and voice with guitar chords.

ANTHOLOGY OF BROADWAY SONGS – GOLD EDITION

100 beloved songs from the Great White Way, including: All I Ask of You • Day by Day • Good Morning Baltimore • Guys and Dolls • It's De-Lovely • Makin' Whoopee! • My Favorite Things • On the Street Where You Live • Send in the Clowns • They Call the Wind Maria • Written in the Stars • Younger Than Springtime • and more.
00311954 P/V/G $24.99

ANTHOLOGY OF CHRISTMAS SONGS – GOLD EDITION

A cream-of-the-crop collection of 100 holiday favorites, both secular and sacred, including: All I Want for Christmas Is You • Carol of the Bells • Dance of the Sugar Plum Fairy • The First Noel • Jingle-Bell Rock • Joy to the World • O Christmas Tree • Santa Baby • Up on the Housetop • What Child Is This? • and more.
00311998 P/V/G $24.99

ANTHOLOGY OF COUNTRY SONGS – GOLD EDITION

100 of the best country songs ever: Always on My Mind • Butterfly Kisses • Coal Miner's Daughter • I Will Always Love You • Jackson • Mountain Music • Ring of Fire • Rocky Top • Take Me Home, Country Roads • Through the Years • Whiskey River • You Are My Sunshine • and scores more!
00312052 P/V/G $24.99

ANTHOLOGY OF JAZZ SONGS – GOLD EDITION

This solid collection of jazz favorites boasts 100 songs that set the gold standard for jazz classics! Includes: All of You • April in Paris • Come Fly with Me • From This Moment On • I Got It Bad and That Ain't Good • In the Mood • Lazy River • St. Louis Blues • Stormy Weather (Keeps Rainin' All the Time) • When I Fall in Love • and dozens more.
00311952 P/V/G $24.99

ANTHOLOGY OF LATIN SONGS – GOLD EDITION

100 Latin-flavored favorites, including: Bésame Mucho (Kiss Me Much) • Cast Your Fate to the Wind • Desafinado • La Bamba • Mas Que Nada • One Note Samba (Samba De Uma Nota So) • Quiet Nights of Quiet Stars (Corcovado) • So Nice (Summer Samba) • Spanish Eyes • Sway (Quien Sera) • and more.
00311956 P/V/G $24.99

ANTHOLOGY OF LOVE SONGS – GOLD EDITION

This fantastic collection features 100 songs full of love and romance, including: And I Love You So • Cheek to Cheek • Crazy • Fields of Gold • Grow Old with Me • Just the Way You Are • Love Me Tender • On a Slow Boat to China • Take My Breath Away (Love Theme) • A Time for Us (Love Theme) • Unchained Melody • When I Need You • and more.
00311955 P/V/G $24.99

ANTHOLOGY OF MOVIE SONGS – GOLD EDITION

An outstanding collection of favorite cinema songs, including: Bella's Lullaby • Dancing Queen • Georgia on My Mind • I Will Always Love You • Love Story • Mission: Impossible Theme • Theme from The Simpsons • Take My Breath Away (Love Theme) • A Whole New World • You Are the Music in Me • and many more.
00311967 P/V/G $24.99

ANTHOLOGY OF R&B SONGS – GOLD EDITION

100 R&B classics are included in this collection: ABC • Brick House • Get Ready • I Say a Little Prayer • It's Your Thing • Mustang Sally • Please Mr. Postman • Respect • This Old Heart of Mine (Is Weak for You) • What'd I Say • and more.
00312016 P/V/G $24.99

ANTHOLOGY OF ROCK SONGS – GOLD EDITION

This amazing collection features 100 rock hits, including: Africa • Bad, Bad Leroy Brown • Chantilly Lace • December 1963 (Oh, What a Night) • Fun, Fun, Fun • A Hard Day's Night • Layla • Night Moves • Ramblin' Man • That'll Be the Day • We Will Rock You • and many more.
00311953 P/V/G $24.99

FOR MORE INFORMATION, SEE YOUR LOCAL MUSIC DEALER, OR WRITE TO:

HAL•LEONARD® CORPORATION
7777 W. BLUEMOUND RD. P.O. BOX 13819 MILWAUKEE, WI 53213

Visit Hal Leonard Online at
www.halleonard.com

Prices, contents, and availability subject to change without notice.

0111